D1273813

Owls

Are Night Animals

St. John's School Lower Library

by Joanne Mattern

Reading consultant: Susan Nations, M.Ed., author/literacy coach/consultant in literacy development
Science and curriculum consultant: Debra Voege, M.A., science and math curriculum resource teacher

Please visit our web site at: www.garethstevens.com
For a free color catalog describing Weekly Reader® Early Learning Library's list
of high-quality books, call 1-877-445-5824 (USA) or 1-800-387-3178 (Canada).
Weekly Reader® Early Learning Library's fax: (414) 336-0164.

Library of Congress Cataloging-in-Publication Data

Mattern, Joanne, 1963-
 . Owls are night animals / by Joanne Mattern.
     p. cm. — (Night animals)
   Includes bibliographical references and index.
   ISBN-13: 978-0-8368-7848-6 (lib. bdg.)
   ISBN-13: 978-0-8368-7855-4 (softcover)
   1. Owls—Juvenile literature. I. Title.
   QL696.S83M385   2007
   598.9'7—dc22   2006030884

This edition first published in 2007 by
Weekly Reader® Early Learning Library
A Member of the WRC Media Family of Companies
330 West Olive Street, Suite 100
Milwaukee, Wisconsin 53212 USA

Editor: Tea Benduhn
Art direction: Tammy West
Cover design and page layout: Scott M. Krall
Picture research: Diane Laska-Swanke

Picture credits: Cover, title page © Yuri Shibnev/naturepl.com; p. 5 © Raymond Gehman/National Geographic Image
Collection; p. 7 © Tom Vezo/naturepl.com; p. 9 © Tom and Pat Leeson; p. 11 © Kevin J. Keatley/naturepl.com;
p. 13 © Wendy Dennis/Visuals Unlimited; p. 15 © Kim Taylor/naturepl.com; pp. 17, 19 © Joe McDonald/
Visuals Unlimited; p. 21 © Joe & Mary Ann McDonald/Visuals Unlimited

Printed in the United States of America

1 2 3 4 5 6 7 8 9 10 10 09 08 07 06

Note to Educators and Parents

Reading is such an exciting adventure for young children! They are beginning to integrate their oral language skills with written language. To encourage children along the path to early literacy, books must be colorful, engaging, and interesting; they should invite the young reader to explore both the print and the pictures.

The *Night Animals* series is designed to help children read about creatures that are active during the night. Each book explains what a different night animal does during the day, how it finds food, and how it adapts to its nocturnal life.

Each book is specially designed to support the young reader in the reading process. The familiar topics are appealing to young children and invite them to read — and reread — again and again. The full-color photographs and enhanced text further support the student during the reading process.

In addition to serving as wonderful picture books in schools, libraries, homes, and other places where children learn to love reading, these books are specifically intended to be read within an instructional guided reading group. This small group setting allows beginning readers to work with a fluent adult model as they make meaning from the text. After children develop fluency with the text and content, the books can be read independently. Children and adults alike will find these books supportive, engaging, and fun!

— Susan Nations, M.Ed., author/literacy coach/
consultant in literacy development

A spooky **hoot** fills
the night air. Who . . .
Whoo . . . Whooo . . .
do you hear? It is
an owl!

Owls **hunt** at night. They are **carnivores**. Carnivores are animals that eat meat. Owls eat mice and worms and many other kinds of small animals.

Many parts of an owl's body help it hunt. **Feathers** cover its ears, but an owl still has excellent hearing.

An owl can turn its head toward any sound. Its head can turn around very far. An owl can look behind itself. It can even turn its head upside down!

Owls also have very big
eyes. Their eyes help
them see in the dark.
An owl can see a small
animal moving along
the ground.

Owls have thick feathers on their wings. Thick feathers help the owl fly very quietly. An owl can easily sneak up on its **prey**.

Owls have strong claws called **talons**. They reach down and grab prey with their talons. Owls are strong night animals.

talons

When an owl sees prey, it **swoops** down to grab it. Then the owl carries the prey off to eat it.

Whoosh! Swoop! Whooo ... Do you hear the night wind? Look around. It might be an owl.

Glossary

carnivores — animals that eat meat

hunt — to find and kill other animals for food

prey — an animal that is hunted by another animal

swoops — flies downward very quickly

talons — long, sharp claws on a large bird's feet

For More Information

Books

Owls. Animal Kingdom (series). Julie Murray
   (ABDO Publishing)

Owls. Animals That Live in the Forest (series).
   JoAnn Early Macken (Gareth Stevens)

Owls. Woodland Animals (series). Emily Rose Townsend
   (Pebble Books)

Owls: Flat-Faced Flyers. Wild World of Animals (series).
   Adele D. Richardson (Bridgestone Books)

Web Site

All About Owls
www.EnchantedLearning.com/subjects/birds/info/Owl.shtml
Make an owl craft, take a quiz about owls, learn fun facts about
owls, and see some different kinds of owls.

Publisher's note to educators and parents: Our editors have
carefully reviewed this Web site to ensure that it is suitable for children.
Many Web sites change frequently, however, and we cannot guarantee
that a site's future contents will continue to meet our high standards of
quality and educational value. Be advised that children should be closely
supervised whenever they access the Internet.

Index

About the Author

Joanne Mattern has written more than 150 books for children. She has written about unusual animals, sports, history, world cities, and many other topics. Joanne also works in her local library. She lives in New York State with her husband, three daughters, and assorted pets. She enjoys animals, music, reading, going to baseball games, and visiting schools to talk about her books.